Luisa Pérez-Sotelo • Eileen Hogan

The Essential
Spanish
PHRASE BOOK
for Teachers

Communicate With Your
Spanish-Speaking Students
and Their Families—Instantly!

■ SCHOLASTIC

NEW YORK • TORONTO • LONDON • AUCKLAND • SYDNEY
MEXICO CITY • NEW DELHI • HONG KONG • BUENOS AIRES

Dedication

Luisa Pérez-Sotelo

To my dear husband and son, whose unconditional moral
support helped me achieve this life dream.

Eileen Hogan

I wish to dedicate this work to my daughter, Maureen Dobyns,
whose enthusiastic embrace of Spanish has inspired me to learn this
helpful language late in my professional life. She has always patiently
corrected my attempts at speaking Spanish and provided insight
into the process of acquiring a second language. It is because of my
personal struggle to learn another language and my observations
in public schools that I empathize with the children who are
trying to make sense of what is going on.

I would like to thank first my coauthor, Dr. Luisa Pérez-Sotelo, for
suggesting the project and for her tireless work as we collaborated to
complete this book. I also want to thank Lois Bridges, our enthusiastic
editor, for her support throughout the process from proposal to finished
product. I would be remiss if I did not mention Amy Rowe and the
copy editors, Queta Fernandez and Jeannine Hutchins, for their
attention to detail and supportive editing.

Acquisitions editor: Lois Bridges
Production editor: Amy Rowe
Cover designer: Brian LaRossa
Interior designer: Jorge Namerow

ISBN-13: 978-0-545-08243-3
ISBN-10: 0-545-08243-9

Table of Contents

Introduction

Raymundo was nervous and a bit scared. His parents had just brought him to a room in this new school with other kids his size. They all looked around and stared at him as he sat down where a lady pointed for him to go. None of them smiled at him. His mom told him that they would leave him there because he was now old enough to go school. His father told him to be good, listen, and learn everything. His little sister, Alicia, held Mami's hand as she looked back to wave good-bye.

Raymundo guessed that the lady who was talking to all the other kids in the room was the teacher. He felt his tummy get tight, and his eyes watered, just a little—he was a big boy now and *would not* cry! He knew that the teacher was speaking English, but it was SO FAST! He knew how to count and say the colors in English, but he didn't recognize any of the words she was saying. Then she came over to him, bent down, smiled a beautiful smile, and said, "Bienvenido, Raymundo. Soy tu maestra, Señora Bailey." Raymundo began to relax and gave a little smile back. Then Ms. Bailey motioned toward a girl and said, "Ella se llama María. Será tu compañera y te ayudará hoy." Maria smiled at him, patted his shoulder, and began to explain in Spanish what was happening next. Raymundo really smiled now, took a deep breath, and felt that he could get through this first day of kindergarten.

It was Carmen's first month in fifth grade. She came to this school last January and had been learning English along with everything else. She liked her teacher, who was patient and explained things pretty well. She had made some good friends in her class. Some of them talked to her in English, and some could speak Spanish. She thought she could speak English okay now, but when she had to write or explain something, it always sounded wrong or different to her ears. Some of the kids who weren't her friends would snicker at her attempts, so she usually didn't want to answer any of the teacher's questions out loud. Today she was feeling okay because she had on one of her new outfits. It was just like her friend's, so she knew she fit in. As the day wore on, she began to ache and feel pains down below her stomach. She put her head down on her desk . . . Then she realized—her period was starting AGAIN. She had had it only about four other times, and Mami said that she wouldn't know when it was going to happen for a while. OH MY GOSH! She wondered, What am I going to do . . . I am not prepared! The teacher came over and said very quietly, "Carmen, ¿estás bien? Parece que te sientes mal. ¿Estás con la regla?" Carmen whispered "Sí," knowing that no one around her could understand Spanish. She was so grateful to her teacher for noticing. She left to go to the nurse for supplies.

These two children represent thousands of others who face similar and even more confusing or private problems every day throughout the country. How wonderful it would be if each teacher could communicate with them briefly in their own language so that they could feel more at ease and welcome in the classroom as they try to learn English and everything else required in today's schools.

The goal of this bilingual (English/Spanish) guide for elementary school teachers (pre-K through 6) in the United States is to help improve communication between Hispanic students and their families, whose first language is Spanish, and school administrators, teachers, and staff.

In addition to grammar and typical language explanations in Spanish as a second-language text, this guide lets teachers quickly find the section that covers the situation at hand and have something helpful to say. The chapters are arranged in three sections: Inside the Classroom, Inside the School, and Inside Family Communication. Topics vary from the first day of school to calls to parents to the use of an interpreter in family conferences.

The chapters contain bilingual tables, useful idiomatic expressions, cognates (synonyms that are very similar in spelling and pronunciation in both languages), and vocabulary pertinent to diverse topics that often come up in classroom conversations. This short book consists of eight chapters following a thematic approach and covering typical situations and events in an elementary school day. In addition, in Chapter 8, there are explanations of how to respect the need for privacy and communicate concern to the preadolescent student who may be dealing with emotional and physical issues. Each chapter begins with a topic and a dialogue table followed by a list of useful expressions, structure, and grammatical explanations, including verb conjugations, vocabulary focusing on cognates, cultural presentations, and common structures. ¡Ojo! sections are also included for extra grammar clarification. Ojo literally means "eye", but it is also used to mean "Notice this" Teachers can make use of this while teaching so that the Spanish speakers know that they need to pay close attention to a particular point. For example: "¡Ojo! Here is the list for homework tonight." Each chapter contains a short explanation of Hispanic culture in general, as it relates to behavior in school. The appendix contains a cognate list.

This guide has been developed in response to teachers' urgent need to communicate with their newly arrived Spanish-speaking students. We use a communicative, inductive approach, where everyday language and diverse content and structures are introduced in meaningful contexts and situations. Different ways of communicating the same idea are presented in the chapters, and vocabulary is repeated in some of the tables, with the objective of helping you understand the language as we repeat common and useful words and expressions. Also, diverse tenses and grammar are included in the tables, but not in traditional textbook order since natural learning not occurs in that way (Lee & Van Patten, 2003) but as needed, during different types of real rather than forced conversations.

Spanish is a phonetic language; in other words, it is pronounced as it is written. Consequently, teachers will be able to pronounce new phrases correctly just by learning how to pronounce Spanish vowels, because Spanish words are phonetically regular. Unlike English, there are almost no alternative pronunciations in Spanish.

It is important to remember that there are, of course, several Spanish dialects, with different preferences in pronunciations and word choices. Dr. Luisa Pérez-Sotelo, who wrote all the Spanish in this book, was born in Perú and is a native Spanish speaker. However, she has been teaching Spanish as a second language here in the United States since 1989 using standard Spanish language textbooks. Therefore, she describes her dialect as a mix of Latin American and Spanish (Spain) influences. Those teachers who have students from the Dominican Republic, Puerto Rico, and Cuba will hear different pronunciations, words, and expressions. Also, people in Argentina and Paraguay use different stress rules for commands. Dr. Pérez-Sotelo has tried to use grammar and vocabulary accepted by the Real Academia de la Lengua Española and urges teachers to find the pertinent alternatives for their own students.

We hope that you will find this book easy to use and effective in helping you communicate with children like Raymundo and Carmen and with their parents. Our goal as educators is to help our students achieve their potential as competent people and active citizens, and we offer this book to help in that effort.

Inside Spanish Phonetics

According to John Dalbor (1997), "there is a close and consistent correspondence between the written symbols and the sounds they stand for in the Spanish spelling system" (p.2).

Spanish Vowels

There are five vowels in the Spanish language—a, e, i, o, u—and they are always pronounced in the same way. For example:

papá
Pepe
pipo
poco
puna

In other words, the *a* in *papá* is the same *a* as in all the words that contain an *a* and the same occurs with the other four vowels. That's why Spanish is so easy to pronounce and is called a phonetic language. The vowels do not vary according to words or word environment as they do in English. For example, the letter *a* in the word *table* is pronounced in one way, while *a* in *dad* is pronounced in a totally different way.

Spanish Consonants and Digraphs That Differ From English

There are a few consonants in Spanish that differ from English. However, if the English native speaker mispronounces them, the Spanish native speaker still understands. For example, the letter *v* does not have the distinctive *v* sound as in English. Spanish speakers pronounce the written *v* like a *b*. There's also a trilled *rr* in Spanish that does not exist in English, like in the Spanish word *carro*. The *ñ* in Spanish is pronounced as an *n* followed by a *y*, as in the English *canyon—cañón* in Spanish. The double *ll* in Spanish is pronounced as a *y*. For instance, the word *llamo* is phonetically described as /yamo/ rather than /lamo/. Note: *rr* and *ll* as well as *ch* are not considered letters but digraphs. These digraphs have traditionally also been treated as letters of the alphabet. However, when used at the beginning of the sentence, capitalize only the first, so it's *Chillón* not *CHillón*. If there is a Spanish alphabet chart in the room, *ch*, *rr*, and *ll* will be separate letters. Also, in Spanish there is no /z/ sound even though some words are written with *z*. In Latin America the *z* is pronounced as *s*. In contrast, the *z* in northern and central

Spain is pronounced like the *th* in the American English phrase *thank*. We consider these to be the main differences between Spanish and English consonants. You may find additional differences in a phonetics course.

What About Cognates?

Spanish cognates (words that have a common origin) are an integral part of developing a Spanish vocabulary. Many words in Spanish resemble words in English and provide a quick source of building a strong Spanish vocabulary. However, not all words that sound alike in Spanish and English have the same meaning. For more information on cognates, visit the Colorín Colorado Web site: www.colorincolorado.org/educators/background/cognates, and, for list of cognates, www.colorincolorado.org/pdfs/articles/cognates.pdf.

Here are some examples of common English/Spanish cognates:

Nouns		Verbs	
babies	bebés	adopt	adoptar
blouse	blusa	discuss	discutir
chocolate	chocolate	introduce	introducir
computers	computadoras	respond	responder
day	día		
list	lista	**Adjectives**	
music	música	flexible	flexible
pants	pantalones	important	importante
plates	platos	miniature	miniatura
sweater	suéter	terrible	terrible

CHAPTER 1

SURVIVING THE FIRST DAY OF SCHOOL

(at the beginning of the school year or
whinever a student joins the class)

While this guide will help you with the immediate challenges of communicating with your Spanish-speaking students, we hope you'll take time to learn more about the process of second language acquisition in general. In the very helpful article "Extending English-Language Learners' Classroom Interactions Using the Response Protocol," by Kathleen and Eric Mohr (2007), the authors explain the cultural differences that many immigrant children bring to school in the United States in regard to answering and asking questions. Typically, schools outside of the United States give the teachers an elevated status that requires the students to listen rather than talk. In contrast, teachers in the U.S. ask many questions and expect the students to participate in discussion when appropriate. The Mohrs' article provides several recommended practices to improve all students' knowledge and advocates the use of what they call academic language in the classroom. We recommend that readers of this book refer to this article, as well as other articles and books on teaching English language learners.

A Note About Language and Culture
Pronouncing Your Students' Names

Try very hard to pronounce the student's name correctly. It is so important for a new student to feel welcome. Spanish names are phonetically regular. Unlike English, there are no alternative pronunciations. It is considered impolite to "Americanize" a child's name. Avoid saying Mary for Maria or John for Juan, George for Jorge, Susan for Susana, Rose for Rosa, Michael for Miguel, and so on.

Respect for Teachers

As a sign of respect in Spain, Mexico, Ecuador, Perú, Colombia, Venezuela, and in most Latin American countries, students usually look down when a person in authority speaks to them. However, American teachers might misunderstand this as not paying attention or as showing disrespect. In Perú and Mexico for example, students hold teachers in high regard and think they should not speak up in class; therefore, they seldom ask questions or challenge the teacher. Also, in South America students typically stand when talking to the teacher, while American students do not.

PART I: INSIDE THE CLASSROOM

Welcome to Class

How to address one student:

Good morning, I am -------, your teacher.	Buenos días, soy ------- tu maestro/maestra.
What is your name?	¿Cómo te llamas?
I am from Kansas. Where are you from?	Soy de Kansas. ¿Y tú, de dónde eres?
I am from Monterey.	Soy de Monterey.
I am so happy that you will be in my class this year!	¡Estoy feliz de tenerte en mi clase este año!
Come in, your seat is right here.	Ven, tu asiento está aquí.
This is _____. She/he will be your buddy to help you today.	Él/ella se llama _____y será el/la compañero/compañera que te ayudará hoy.

Language Structure: Verb Conjugations in the Present Tense

When a verb is used in a sentence, the verb ending has to agree with its subject.

Ser (to be) is used to express professions, time, personality traits, physical characteristics, origin, days of the week.

yo soy (I am) **nosotros somos** (we are)
tú eres (you are) **vosotros sois** (you are)
él/ella/usted/esto es (he/she/you/it is) **ellos/ellas/ustedes son** (they/you are)

Important: In Spanish, you may omit the subject pronouns (yo, tú, él, nosotros, etc.) because the verb form tells which subject you are referring to. From now on, we will only present the verb form without its respective subject pronoun.

Estar (to be) is used to express location and emotions.

estoy estamos
estás estáis
está están

Llamarse (to be called)

When a verb ends in se, it is called a reflexive verb and it needs to be conjugated with the reflexive pronouns me, te, se, nos, os, se with the verb form.

me llamo	nos llamamos
te llamas	os llamáis
se llama	se llaman

 ¡Ojo! When a verb ends in *se*, it is called a "reflexive verb," and it is necessary to conjugate it with an attached reflexive pronoun; for instance, *ponme, ponte* in affirmative commands. The pronoun is placed before the verb in negative commands: no te pongas.

Other verbs that are used in this way are: *ducharse* (to shower), *cepillarse los dientes* (to brush one's teeth), *peinarse* (to comb one's hair), *vestirse* (to get dressed), *alistarse* (to get ready), *bañarse* (to bathe oneself), *mirarse* (to look at oneself), *herirse* (to hurt oneself), *caerse* (to fall), *dañarse* (to get damaged), *sentarse* (to sit down), *sentirse* (to feel), *levantarse* (to get up), *despertarse* (to wake up), etc.

Classroom Routines

How to address one student:

Please speak louder and respond in class.	Habla más recio/fuerte y responde en clase, por favor.
It is time to stand in line with the other kids/boys/girls.	Es la hora de ponerse en fila con los otros niños/otras niñas.
It is time for lunch.	Es la hora del almuerzo.
This is where you will put your coat and backpack.	Aquí vas a poner tu chaqueta y tu mochila.
It is time to go to the bathroom.	Es la hora de ir al baño.
It is time for recess.	Es la hora del recreo.

How to address more than one student (verb forms change):

Please speak louder and respond in class.	Hablen más recio/fuerte y respondan en clase, por favor.
It is time to stand in line.	Es la hora de ponerse en fila.
This is where you will put your coats and backpacks.	Aquí van a poner sus chaquetas y sus mochilas.
It is time for lunch.	Es la hora de almorzar.
It is time to go to the bathroom.	Es la hora de ir al baño.
It is time for recess.	Es la hora de ir al recreo.

¡Ojo! Regular verbs like *hablar* are conjugated with the following endings: **o, as, a, amos, áis, an** in the present tense.

Language Structure: Conjugation of Regular "Ar" Verbs in the Present Tense

hablar	**(to speak)**
habl**o**	habl**amos**
habl**as**	habl**áis**
habl**a**	habl**an**

Ex: Hablamos inglés y español aquí. *We speak Spanish and English here.*

The following common *ar* verbs are conjugated in the same way as the verb *hablar* above.

answer **contestar**	*arrive* **llegar**
buy **comprar**	*carry* **llevar**
clean **limpiar**	*call* **llamar**
converse **conversar**	*color* **colorear**
draw **dibujar**	*delete* **borrar**
evacuate **evacuar**	*encourage* **animar**
escalate **escalar**	*explain* **explicar**
fight **pelear**	*fix* **arreglar**
have dinner **cenar**	*have breakfast* **desayunar**
invite **invitar**	*leave behind* **dejar**
look at **mirar**	*listen to* **escuchar**
look for **buscar**	*need* **necesitar**
plan **planear**	*practice* **practicar**
prepare **preparar**	*push* **empujar**
rest **descansar**	*return* **regresar**
study **estudiar**	*sing* **cantar**
steal **robar**	*swim* **nadar**
take **tomar**	*teach* **enseñar**
throw away **botar/tirar**	*travel* **viajar**
visit **visitar**	*walk* **caminar**
wash **lavar**	*wait* **esperar**
wish **desear**	*work* **trabajar**

Language Structure: How to Ask a Question in Spanish

To ask a question, place the verb in front of the subject. In the written form, the inverted question mark is in front of the sentence, as below.

Example:

¿Hablas español? *Do you speak Spanish?*
¿Hablan español en tu casa? *Do all of you speak Spanish at home?*
Negation in Spanish: to say a negative sentence, place the word "no" before the verb.

Example:

El/ella no contesta la pregunta. *He/She does not answer the question.*
Pedro no llega tarde a clase. *Pedro does not arrive late to class.*

To answer a question in the negative form, "no" is used twice in the negative response:

¿Llamas a tu hermano? *Do you call your brother?*
No, no lo llamo. *No, I don't call him.*

Teacher Note About Language and Culture:
The Difference Between "Tú" and "Usted" ("You")

Unlike English, there are two forms of *you* in Spanish, one, is familiar or informal, and the other, *usted*, is formal. *Tú* is used to address students, friends, and family members. However, in some regions, children use *usted* to address their parents. *Usted* is also used to address an authority figure such as your doctor, your teacher, your dentist, the principal, and older people in general. When writing, *usted* has the contracted form *Ud*.

It is important to mention that these days people often use *tú* in place of *usted*, especially in some Hispanic regions, such as Perú, Chile, and Paraguay. Furthermore, *tú* is used with the second person singular of the verb form, while *usted* is used with the third person singular. The plural form of *tú* and *usted* is *ustedes*.

Example:

How to address a parent:
Usted **tiene** cuatro niños, no? *You have four children, right?*
How to address a student:
Tú **tienes** dos hermanos, no? *You have two brothers, right?*
How to address more than one person, formally or informally:
Ustedes trabajan en el centro ¿no? *You guys work downtown, right?*

Communicating With Parents

How to convey general instructions and questions to parents:

This is the list of supplies that we will need for this class.	Esta es la lista de materiales que se necesitan en la clase.
You need to purchase them as soon as possible.	Deben comprarlos tan pronto como sea posible.
What do you call him/her at home?	¿Cómo lo/la llaman en casa?
What should we call him/her here at school?	¿Cómo lo/la debemos llamar aquí en la escuela?
Let me practice. (Repeat the name.) Is that close? Correct?	Permítanme practicar (pronunciar el nombre). ¿Está bien?

Language Structure: Conjugation of Regular "Er" Verbs in the Present Tense

Comer (to eat)

com**o**	com**emos**
com**es**	com**éis**
com**e**	com**en**

In Spanish, verbs ending in "er" have the following endings when conjugated:

o, es, e, emos, éis, en.

The following verbs are conjugated in the same way:

believe **creer**	drink **beber**
learn **aprender**	read **leer**
respond **responder**	un **correr**
should/ought to/must **deber**	understand **comprender**

Verb + infinitive

An already conjugated verb is followed by the base form (infinitive) of the verb (without conjugation).

Debo llamar. I should call. **Deben comprar.** You/they should buy/.

¿Necesitas comer? Do you need to eat?

Language Structure: Conjugation of Regular "Ir" Verbs in the Present Tense

Vivir (to live)

viv**o**	viv**imos**
viv**es**	viv**ís**
viv**e**	viv**en**

Regular verbs ending in "ir" have the following endings:
o, es, e, imos, ís, en.

allow **permitir**		*attend* **asistir**	
decide **decidir**		*describe* **describir**	
open **abrir**		*receive* **recibir**	
share **compartir**		*write* **escribir**	

Expressions of Frequency in the Present Tense

every day **todos los días**	*every other day* **dejando un día es**
often **con frecuencia**	*usually* **generalmente**
sometimes **a veces**	*seldom* **rara vez**

Vocabulary
Numbers - Números

1 uno	un libro	(book)
2 dos	dos cuadernos	(notebooks)
3 tres	tres papeles	(papers)
4 cuatro	cuatro colores	(colors)
5 cinco	cinco niños	(boys)
6 seis	seis mesas	(tables)
7 siete	siete lápices	(pencils)
8 ocho	ocho niñas	(girls)
9 nueve	nueve sillas	(chairs)
10 diez	diez mochilas	(backpacks)
11 once	once paraguas	(umbrellas)
12 doce	doce gatos	(cats)
13 trece	trece bebés	(babies)

14 catorce	catorce bebidas	(drinks)
15 quince	quince platos	(plates)
16 dieciséis	dieciséis vasos	(glasses/cups)
17 diecisiete	diecisiete servilletas	(napkins)
18 dieciocho	dieciocho chocolates	(chocolates)
19 diecinueve	diecinueve dulces	(sweets)
20 veinte	veinte bolsas de palomitas	(bags of popcorn)

Colors - Colores

red	rojo	I have a red blouse.	Tengo una blusa roja.
blue	azul	You have a blue jacket.	Tú tienes una chaqueta azul.
yellow	amarillo	She has a yellow ribbon.	Ella tiene una cinta amarilla.
green	verde	He has a green cap.	El tiene una gorra verde.
brown	marrón	We have brown shoes.	Nosotros tenemos zapatos marrones.
black	negro	They have black pants.	Ellos/ellas tienen pantalones negros.
white	blanco	I have white socks.	Tengo medias blancas.
pink	rosado	You have a pink skirt.	Usted tiene/tú tienes una falda rosada.
orange	anaranjado	He has an orange sweater.	El tiene un suéter anaranjado.

 ¡Ojo! The color orange can also be translated as **naranja**. The color brown can also be translated as **café**.

Language Structure: Conjugation of the Irregular Verb "tener" in the Present Tense

Tener *(to have)*

ten**go**	tenemos
ti**e**nes	tenéis
ti**e**ne	ti**e**nen

The Essential Spanish Phrase Book for Teachers

The verbs *tener* and *venir* are very similar when conjugated. They both use a *g* in the first person singular and they change the stem *e* to *ie* in the second person singular and the third person singular and plural.

Venir *(to come)*

ven**g**o	venimos
v**ie**nes	venís
v**ie**ne	v**ie**nen

 ¡Ojo! The *nosotros* and *vosotros* subject pronouns (first and second person plural do not change stems).

Language Structure: Conjugation of Irregular Verbs in the First Person Singular in the Present

Hacer *(to do/to make)*		**poner** *(to put)*		**salir** *(to leave/to go out)*	
ha**g**o	hacemos	pon**g**o	ponemos	sal**g**o	salimos
haces	hacéis	pones	ponéis	sales	salís
hace	hacen	pone	ponen	sale	salen

The verb "ir" is an irregular verb

Ir (to go)

voy (I go)	**vamos** (we go)
vas (you go)	**vais** (you go, pl.)
Va (he/she/it goes)	**van** (they/you go, pl.)

Future tense

This verb can also be used to form the future tense. The verb *ir* is used as an auxiliary verb and the main verb is used in the infinitive or base form.

Voy a subir al autobús.	*I am going to get on the bus.*
Vas a escribir.	*You are going to write.*
Va a traer el libro.	*He/she is going to bring the book.*
Vamos a tajar los lápices.	*We're going to sharpen pencils.*
Vais a ir al baño.	*You're going to go to the restroom.*
Van a almorzar.	*They are going to have lunch.*

Remember, the verb *ser* in the first person singular has this form: *soy*, similar to *voy*. These two verbs are similar only in the first person singular. The same happens with the verb *dar* = to give.

Dar *(to give)*

doy	damos
das	dáis
da	dan

Language Structure: Conjugation of Stem-changing Verbs

In these verbs, the main vowel stem changes in the following ways.

e-ie,		o-ue,		e-i	
pensar	*(to think)*	**recordar**	*(to remember)*	**pedir**	*(to order/ask)*
pienso	pensamos	recuerdo	recordamos	pido	pedimos
piensas	pensáis	recuerdas	recordáis	pides	pedís
piensa	piensan	recuerda	recuerdan	pide	piden

e-ie verbs	o-ue verbs	e-i verbs
comenzar *begin*	**poder** *be able*	**pedir** *ask for*
cerrar *close*	**contar** *count*	**seguir** *follow*
perder *close*	**encontrar** *find*	**conseguir** *get*
preferir *prefer*	**almorzar** *have lunch*	**repetir** *repeat*
pensar *think*	**recordar** *remember*	**decir** *say*
entender *understand*	**dormir** *sleep*	**retornar** *return*
querer *want/love*		**mostrar** *show*

!Ojo! When the verb has two identical vowels, such as *preferir*, choose the second one for the stem change-

> prefiero, prefieres, prefiere, prefieren.

With the verb *repetir*:

> repito, repites, repite, repiten.

However, with *perder* or *querer*, use the first e for the stem change:

> **pie**rdo, **pie**rdes, **pie**rde, **pie**rden
> and quiero, quieres, quiere, quieren.

The stem change does not occur in the *nosotros* or *vosotros* form.

A Note About the Spanish Alphabet - El Alfabeto

A B (be) C (ce) Ch (che) D (de) **E** F (efe) G (ge) H (ache) **I** J (jota) K (ca) L (ele) LL (eye) M (eme) N (ene) Ñ (eñe) **O** P (pe) Q (cu) R (ere) RR (erre) S (ese) T (te) **U** V (ve) W (doble ve) X (equis) Y (i griega) Z (ceta).

CHAPTER 2

PROVIDING BASIC CLASSROOM INSTRUCTIONS

You'll want to be especially kind and encouraging with your English-language learners; see Mohr & Mohr, 2007 for helpful suggestions.

Introducing Your Students to Classroom Life
Promoting Understanding and Encouraging Participation

Help me understand what you mean.	Ayúdame a comprender lo que quieres decir.
Tell me again.	¿Qué?
Tell me what you are thinking.	Dime lo que estás pensando.
Do you know any words in English to say that?	¿Sabes cómo decirlo en inglés?
Do you think it is _____ or _____?	¿Piensas que es _____ o _____?
Yes! That's it. Good thinking and good English!	Sí, ¡eso es! Bien pensado y buen inglés!
I think you know something about this.	Creo que tú sabes algo acerca de esto.
I want to hear from you in this lesson.	Quiero escucharte en esta lección.
Get ready with a question or an answer.	Prepara una pregunta o una respuesta.
Good learners ask lots of questions.	Los estudiantes buenos hacen muchas preguntas.
Be thinking, because everyone will get to answer.	Ve pensando porque todos responderán.

Beginning the Day
How to address more than one student:

Hang up your coats and sit down please.	Cuelguen sus abrigos y siéntense por favor.
Please pass out these papers.	Pasen estos papeles, por favor.
These are instructions for buying school supplies for class.	Estas son las instrucciones para comprar los materiales escolares.
Ms. Atkins, Ana doesn't have the paper.	Señorita Atkins, Ana no tiene el papel.
Okay, put the papers away and give them to your parents when you get home.	Bueno, guarden los papeles y se los entregan a sus padres cuando lleguen a casa.

Language Structure: Imperative Mood (Commands)
Formal imperative mood

To give formal commands, we use the subjunctive form of the verb by switching endings. We give formal commands to adults we hardly know or to older people.

Example:

When addressing only one person | When addressing more than one

hablar *(to speak)*
hab**le**   hab**len**

comer *(eat)*
com**a**   com**an**

escribir *(write)*
escrib**a**   escrib**an**

Commands with irregular verb forms:

salir – **salga**	tener – **tenga**	decir – **diga**	ir – **vaya**	saber – **sepa**
venir – **venga**	ser – **sea**	hacer – **haga**	poner – **ponga**	

An easy way to remember these forms is by remembering the present tense first person singular. And change the o to an *a*.

Example:

Present Indicative   **Present Subjunctive**
tengo   tenga

salgo	salga
digo	diga
pongo	ponga
vengo	venga
hago	haga

Saber, ser, and *ir* are unique.

Present Indicative	Present Subjunctive
sé	sepa
soy	sea
voy	vaya

Informal imperative mood

When we give informal commands we address only one person. We give informal commands to children, friends, or peers. We use the third person singular of the verb in the present indicative. For example:

Regular verbs:

hablar	comer	escribir
habla	come	escribe

Irregular verbs have special forms:

salir – **sal**	tener – **ten**	decir – **di**	ir – **ve**
venir – **ven**	ser – **sé**	hacer – **haz**	poner – **pon**

Negative form

For the negative form, the subjunctive mood is used (verb switching) for regular verbs:

hablar	comer	escribir
no habl**es**	no com**as**	no escrib**as**

It is necessary to remember the subjunctive forms for irregular verbs:

no **salgas**	no **tengas**	no **digas**	no **vayas**
no **vengas**	no **seas** o	no **hagas**	no **pongas**

Routines Across the Day
The Read-Aloud

Today, we are going to read the story of___.	Hoy, vamos a leer el cuento de___.
Sit here in a circle please.	Siéntense en círculo, por favor.
Listen well.	Escuchen bien.

Now, answer my questions.	Ahora, respondan a mis preguntas.
What happened next?	¿Qué pasó después?
Who are the characters?	¿Quiénes son los personajes?
Where are they living?	¿Dónde viven ellos?
What happened in the end?	¿Qué pasó al final?

Test-Taking

We have a test today.	Tenemos un examen hoy.
Take out your pencils.	Saquen sus lápices.
Write your name on the paper.	Escriban su nombre en el papel.
Write the answers now.	Escriban las respuestas ahora.
When you are finished, raise your hand, but don't get up.	Cuando terminen, levanten la mano, pero no se levanten.
Ana and Carmen, come to the chalkboard.	Ana y Carmen, vengan a la pizarra.
Write the answers on the board.	Escriban las respuestas en la pizarra.

Recess

Don't run.	No corras.
Don't push.	No empujes.
Don't throw dirt at your classmates.	No les tires tierra a tus compañeros.
Keep the ball inside the fence. (To clarify, Spanish translation means: Don't throw the ball outside of the fence.)	No tires la pelota fuera de la reja.
Line up when you hear the bell.	Ponte en fila cuando oigas la campana.
We will get a drink when we go inside.	Tomaremos una bebida adentro.

Language Structure: Informal Affirmative and Negative Commands

Affirmative (indicative)		Negative (subjunctive)
correr *(to run)*	corre	no corras
dejar *(to leave something, to allow)*	deja	no dejes
empujar *(to push)*	empuja	no empuj<u>es</u>
tirar *(to throw)*	tira	no tires
ponerse en fila *(to get in line)*	ponte en fila	no te pongas en fila

Reflexive Pronouns

me (me)	nos (us)
te (you)	os (you)
se (you, he, she, it)	se (they, you /pl./)

General Classroom Instructions
Classroom Courtesy
How to address one student:

Don't throw trash on the floor.	No botes papeles al suelo
There is a trash can in the corner.	Hay un basurero en el rincón.
Don't yell, please.	No grites, por favor.
Watch your language.	No se dicen malas palabras.
Be polite. Open the door for your classmate.	Sé cortés. Abrele la puerta a tu compañera/compañero.

End of the School Day
How to address more than one student:

When we give a command to only one person, it is important to know the difference in structure between formal and informal commands; however, there is only one form when addressing more than one person.

Put on your jackets.	Pónganse las chaquetas.
Line up and walk to the bus.	Pónganse en fila y caminen hacia el autobús.
It's time to leave now; get your jackets and backpacks.	Es hora de salir. Cojan sus chaquetas y mochilas.

Classroom Vocabulary

You may hear different words depending on where your Spanish-speaking students are from; for example, the word *bus* has different translations in Spanish countries, according to the region. One word is *camión* in Mexico, *gua gua* in some Caribbean countries, *autobús* in Spain and in most Latin American countries, *bus* in Paraguay and Uruguay, and *ómnibus* in Ecuador and Perú.

Daily Action Words

to finish	terminar	Did you finish?	¿Terminaste?
to sit	sentarse	Sit down.	Siéntate.
to get up	levantarse	Get up.	Levántate.
to bring	traer	Bring your paper.	Trae tu papel.
to draw	dibujar	Draw your family.	Dibuja a tu familia.
to think	pensar	Think carefully.	Piensa bien.
to be over	se acabó	The movie is over.	Se acabó la película.
to raise the hand.	levantar la mano	Raise your leg.	Levanta la pierna.
to write	escribir	Write on the board.	Escribe en la pizarra.
to work	trabajar	Work with your classmate.	Trabaja con tu compañero/a.
to have	tener	Do you have a tissue?	¿Tienes papel?
to put/place	poner	Place your books there.	Pon los libros allí.

to hang up the coat/jacket	colgar el abrigo/la chaqueta
to put on the jacket	ponerse la chaqueta
to line up	ponerse en fila
to come to class	venir a clase
to get/to catch the bus	coger el autobús
to pass papers around	pasar papeles
to have instructions	tener instrucciones
to buy supplies	comprar materiales

to have a piece of paper	tener papel
to put papers away	guardar papeles
to give/to turn in a test	entregar el examen
to arrive at home	llegar a casa
to walk outside	caminar afuera
to run fast	correr rápido
to throw trash	botar la basura

Classroom Materials

paper	papel
pencil	lapiz
ten	bolígrafo
markers	plumones
colors	colores
book	libro

Language Structure: Indefinite Articles

Use the indefinite article *un* in front of a singular indefinite noun and *unos* in front of plural indefinite nouns. *Una* and *unas* are used in front of singular and plural feminine nouns respectively.

un papel	**unos** papeles
una mesa	**unas** mesas

Cognates
Nouns

bus	bus/autobús	poem	poema
circle	círculo	photos	fotos
diary	diario	story	historia
folder	carpeta	Verbs	
instructions	instrucciones		
language	lenguaje	terminated	terminado/da
order	orden	pass out	pasar
permission	permiso		

Understanding Classroom Community
Social Challenges

Here we are supportive of each other.	Aquí todos nos ayudamos.
We avoid insults, put-downs, and threats.	Evitamos insultos, fastidios y amenazas.
If you feel threatened or uneasy, let me know.	Si te sientes amenazado/a o incómodo/a, dímelo.
The younger children look up to you to set a good example.	Los niños de menor edad te miran con respeto y quieren seguir tu ejemplo.
You are ladies and gentlemen. Speak moderately and politely to each other.	Ustedes son damas y caballeros. Hablen con respeto y cortesía.
Always try to find something nice to say to each other.	Siempre traten de decirse algo agradable.
If someone insults/hurts you, let me know and I will deal with it privately.	Si alguien les insulta o hiere, díganmelo y lo trataré de resolver en privado.
We work in groups often in our classroom—the students will help you.	Con frecuencia trabajamos en grupos en la clase—los estudiantes te ayudarán.
I know you are working hard to understand.	Sé que estás haciendo un esfuerzo por comprender.
Be patient, I know you can do it!	Ten paciencia. ¡Sé que puedes hacerlo!
Can you write it down in Spanish or English?	¿Puedes escribirlo en español o en inglés?
I will figure it out.	Ya me daré cuenta.

Peer Pressure

Do you feel sad/upset/embarrassed?	¿Te sientes triste/fastidiado/a, avergonzado/a
How do you feel?	¿Cómo te sientes?
Do you have friends in this class?	¿Tienes amigos/amigas en esta clase?
Who do you hang out with during recess?	¿Con quién te juntas durante el recreo?

Health and Neatness

Did you eat all your lunch?	¿Te comes todo tu almuerzo?
Is there something you don't like to eat?	¿Hay algo que no te gusta comer?
Students need to come to class very clean and wear appropriate clothing.	Los estudiantes deben venir a clase muy limpios y deben usar ropa apropiada.

Cultural Interests

It is interesting to listen or read about other cultures.	Es interesante escuchar o leer acerca de otras culturas.
Can you tell me something interesting about your culture?	¿Puedes decirme algo interesante acerca de tu cultura?

Sports

Get involved in sports to feel better about your mind and body.	Participa en deportes para sentirte mejor mental y físicamente.
What is your favorite sport?	¿Cuál es tu deporte favorito?
Who is your favorite team/player?	¿Cuál es tu equipo/jugador favorito?

Independence

Don't do anything that you will regret later on.	No hagas nada de lo que te puedas arrepentir después.
Behave like a young adult.	Compórtate como un joven adulto.
Many things are not allowed in school. That includes weapon such as knives, box knives, guns, toy guns, fireworks, matches, lighters, and other substances such as tobacco and drugs of any kind.	Hay muchas cosas que no se permiten en la escuela. Eso incluye armas: cuchillos, cuchillas, pistolas, pistolas de juguete, fuegos artificiales, fósforos, encendedores y otras sustancias como tabaco y drogas de todo tipo.

CHAPTER 3

FINE-TUNING CLASSROOM MANAGEMENT

Instructions and Praise

How to address one student:

Remember to do all the parts.	Acuérdate de hacerlo todo.
Hey, great job!	¡Muy bien hecho!
I like that you are cooperating.	Me gusta que cooperes.
Remember to do your best.	Recuerda de hacerlo lo mejor que puedas.
Talk to your partners about it. Very good!	Conversa con tus compañeros/ compañeras acerca de esto. ¡Muy bien!

Language Structure: Verb Conjugation

Gustar (to please) is used in the third person with an indirect object pronoun to mean "to like"

Me gusta	Nos gusta
Te gusta	Os gusta el chocolate (singular)
Le gusta	Les gusta
Me gusta**n**	Nos gusta**n**
Te gusta**n**	Os gusta**n** los chocolates (plural)
Le gusta**n**	Les gusta**n**

Example:

Me gusta la carne.
I like beef.
No me gusta el cerdo.
I don't like pork.

Me gustan las verduras también.
I like vegetables too.
No me gustan los restaurantes de comida rápida.
I don't like fast food restaurants.

This group of verbs behaves like the verb *gustar*:

enojar	*to annoy*
interesar	*to be interested*
molestar	*to bother*
fascinar	*to fascinate*
encantar	*to love /doing/ something*
sorprender	*to get surprised*
importar	*to mind*

It is necessary to use the appropriate indirect object pronoun in front of these verbs, and observe that they are conjugated in a very particular way.

Indirect Object Pronouns

me (me)	nos (us)
te (you)	os (you)
le (him/her/you)	les (them/you)

Work Habits

Working Independently

How to address informal commands to one student:

Do this by yourself.	Hazlo tú solo/sola.
Raise your hand if you have a question.	Levanta la mano si tienes una pregunta.
Do you need help?	¿Necesitas ayuda?
Work carefully.	Trabaja con cuidado.
I knew you could do it!	¡Sabía que lo lograrías!
Good job!	¡Qué bien!
When you finish, read a book and wait for the others.	Cuando termines, lee un libro y espera a los demás.

Questions and Directions

How to address one student:

Do you have your homework?	¿Tienes tu tarea?
Put your books/things away.	Guarda tus libros/cosas.
Show me your note.	Enséñame tu nota.

Discipline Challenges

How to address one student:

Be quiet.	Silencio.
Do you understand the rules?	¿Comprendes las reglas?
Watch me.	Mírame.
Repeat what I say.	Repite.
Don't do that.	No lo hagas.
Don't talk.	No hables.
Lower your voice.	Baja la voz.
Sit down.	Siéntate.
Wait your turn.	Espera tu turno.
Don't touch that.	No lo toques.
Pick it up.	Recógelo.
Where are you going?	¿Adónde vas?
Come stand beside me	Ven y párate junto a mi.
Whose fault is it?	¿De quién es la culpa?
Is your mother at home?	¿Está tu mamá en casa?
I am going to call your parents.	Voy a llamar a tus padres.
I will send a note home.	Voy a mandar una nota a tu casa.

How to address more than one student:

Be quiet.	Silencio.
Do you understand the rules?	¿Comprenden las reglas?
Watch me.	Mírenme.
Repeat what I say.	Repitan.
Don't do that.	No lo hagan.
Don't talk.	No hablen.
Lower your voice.	Bajen la voz.
Sit down.	Siéntense.
Wait your turn.	Esperen su turno.

Don't touch that.	No lo toquen.
Pick it up.	Recójanlo.
Where are you going?	¿Adónde van?
Come stand beside me.	Vengan y párense junto a mí.
Whose fault is it?	¿De quién es la culpa?
Is your mother at home?	¿Están sus mamás en casa?
I am going to call your parents.	Voy a llamar a sus padres.
I will send a note home.	Voy a mandar una nota a sus casas.

Monitoring the Hall

How to address more than one student:

Who is the line leader?	¿Quién es el líder/la líder?
Walk in line.	Caminen en fila.
Hands to yourself.	Sin tocar a nadie.
No running in the hall.	No corran en el pasillo.
Stop at the corner/stairs/door.	Paren en la esquina/en las escaleras, en la puerta.
Wait for them to catch up.	Esperen a los demás.
You have to go to the end.	Tienen que ir a la cola.

Language Structure: Tener que=to have to (showing obligation)

Tengo que hacer mi tarea.	*I have to do my homework.*
Tienes que ir a la cola.	*You have to go to the end.*
Tiene que cortarse las uñas.	*She/He has to cut her/his nails.*
Tenemos que subir al ascensor.	*We have to go on the elevator.*
Tienen que bañarse todos los días.	*They have to bathe every day.*

¡Ojo!
Tener que + infinitive
Tengo que ahorrar = *I have to save*

The same structure is used in English.

Directions Throughout the Day

How to address one student:

Have you finished?	¿Has terminado?
Do you know the answer?	¿Sabes la respuesta?
Pay attention.	Presta atención.
Don't touch it.	No lo toques.
Pick it up.	Recógelo.
Where are you going?	¿Adónde vas?
Watch me.	Mírame.
Be quiet.	Silencio.
Whose?	¿De quién?
Calm down.	Cálmate.
Send _____ home.	Manda a _____ a casa.
Don't touch the screen.	No toques la pantalla.
Watch your teacher.	Mira a tu maestra.
Pick up the paper.	Recoge el papel.
Stand up straight.	Párate derecho/derecha.
Repeat, please.	Repite, por favor.
I don't understand.	No comprendo.
Show me your work.	Enséñame tu trabajo.
Go home now.	Ve a casa ahora.
There is a mistake here.	Hay una falla/un error aquí.
This is your turn.	Te toca a ti.
Help me.	Ayúdame.
Don't speak so loud.	No hables tan fuerte.

Cognates
Nouns

activity	actividad	leader	líder	others	otros
colors	colores	line	línea	turn	turno
problem	problema	note	nota	voice	voz

CHAPTER 4

UNDERSTANDING THE SCHOOL AND SCHEDULES

Language Around the Clock

Morning Routine

How to address more than one student:

Put your things away.	Guarden sus cosas.
Find your journal.	Saquen sus diarios.
Let's do the lunch count.	Contemos el número de almuerzos.
Put your folders in the basket.	Pongan sus carpetas en la canasta.
Good morning.	Buenos días.
It's time for the morning song.	Es hora de cantar.
Did you bring your picture order?	¿Trajeron su orden de fotos?
Do you have your permission slip?	¿Tienen la hojita de permiso?
Where are your coats?	¿Dónde están sus abrigos?
Do you want chocolate milk or plain?	¿Quieren leche con chocolate o blanca?
Before lunch we must go to the bathroom.	Antes de almuerzo debemos ir al baño.
Recess is before math.	El recreo es antes de matemáticas.
Recess is after lunch.	El recreo es después del almuerzo.
We go to computers at 2:00.	Vamos al centro de computadoras a las dos.
Music is on Tuesdays.	Música es los martes.
PE is on Wednesday and Fridays.	Educación física es los miércoles y viernes.
Our schedule today is different.	Nuestro horario de hoy es diferente.
We have these changes.	Hay estos cambios.

Questions and Answers

How to question and address one student:

Did you do your homework last night?	¿Hiciste tu tarea anoche?
It is not in my folder.	No está in mi carpeta
Be sure to look for it and bring it tomorrow.	Asegúrate de buscarla y de traerla mañana.
Can I sharpen my pencil?	¿Puedo sacarle punta a mi lápiz?
Yes, you can. It is the time to do that now.	Sí, puedes. Este es el momento de hacerlo.

Language Structure: *Preterite Past Tense*

Regular verbs are conjugated like this in the past tense:

Hablar	**Comer**	**Escribir**
hab**lé**	com**í**	escrib**í**
hab**laste**	com**iste**	escrib**iste**
hab**ló**	com**ió**	escrib**ió**
hab**lamos**	com**imos**	escrib**imos**
hab**lasteis**	com**isteis**	escrib**isteis**
hab**laron**	com**ieron**	escrib**ieron**

Other regular verbs ending in *ar*: *trabajar, estudiar, cantar, contestar, preguntar*, etc. Check the verb list on page 12 in Chapter 1.

- The preterite endings of regular *er* and *ir* verbs are identical.

- The *nosotros* form of the preterite is identical to the *nosotros* form of the present indicative in regular *ar* and *ir* verbs. The meaning is usually clarified through context.

Examples:

Nosotros **conversamos** todos los días. *We talk every day.* Present

Nosotros **conversamos** ayer. *We talked yesterday.* Past

Spelling Changes

- Verbs ending in *car, gar, guar*, and *zar* have a spelling change in the first person singular:

c–qu	pra**c**ticar	yo practi**qué**	*I practiced*
g–gu	pa**g**ar	yo pa**gué**	*I paid*
z–c	empe**z**ar	yo empe**cé**	*I started*
u–ü	averi**gu**ar	yo averi**güé**	*I found out*

Other verbs that follow these rules:

almorzar	**almorcé** *I had lunch*	**entregar**	**entregué** *I turned in*
sacar	**saqué** *I took out*	**Tocar**	**toqué** *I touched/played*

- Three other verbs: creer, leer, and oir, change the **i** to **y** in the third person singular and plural.

Leer (*to read*)	**Creer** (*to believe*)	**Oir** (*to hear*)
leí	creí	oí
leíste	creíste	oíste
le**y**ó	cre**y**ó	o**y**ó
leímos	creímos	oímos
leísteis	creísteis	oísteis
le**y**eron	cre**y**eron	o**y**eron

- Other verbs in this category: *huir* (to flee), *influir* (to influence), *construir* (to build)

¡Ojo! There are no stem changes for ar and er verbs in the preterite. Only ir verbs change the stem, but not in the same way they do in the present tense. Observe that the stem change is only in the third person singular and plural in the preterite, and the *ue* changes to *u*.

Present **ue**	Past **u**
Dormir *(to sleep)*	
d**ue**rmo	dormí
d**ue**rmes	dormiste
d**ue**rme	d**u**rmió
dormimos	dormimos
dormís	dormisteis
d**ue**rmen	d**u**rmieron

Ir verbs that change from *e* to *i* in the present keep the same change in the preterite, but only in the third person singular and plural.

Pedir (*to order*)		**Conseguir** (*to get*)	
p**i**do	pedí	cons**i**go	conseguí
p**i**des	pediste	cons**i**gues	conseguiste
p**i**de	p**i**dió	cons**i**gue	cons**i**guió
pedimos	pedimos	conseguimos	conseguimos
pedís	pedisteis	conseguís	conseguimos
p**i**den	p**i**dieron	cons**i**guen	cons**i**guieron

Expressions used in the past tense:

Last night	**anoche**	*last year*	**el año pasado**
Last week	**la semana pasada**	*yesterday*	**ayer**
Last month	**el mes pasado**	*day before yesterday*	**antes de ayer**

The Essential Spanish Phrase Book for Teachers

Parts of the School

principal's office	la oficina del director/de la directora
nurse's office	la enfermería
cafeteria	la cafeteria
hallway	el pasillo
bathroom	el baño
gymnasium	el gimnasio
playground	el patio
parking lot	el parqueo
counselor's office	la oficina del consejero/de la consejera
library	la biblioteca
classroom	la clase
computer lab	el centro de computadoras
music room	la sala de música
art room	la sala de arte
science laboratory	el laboratorio de ciencias
front door	la puerta principal
playground door	la puerta del patio

Safety Drills

U.S. schools and communities generally have safety drills and an organized system in place to prepare for and respond to emergencies. America also has more and better resources than many Spanish-speaking countries, where emergency situations may tend to provoke more fear.

Tornado drill—this is practice.	Adiestramiento para tornado—esto es una práctica.
Walk quietly to the hall and sit down.	Caminen al pasillo en silencio y siéntense.
Head down in your lap.	Pongan la cabeza en sus piernas.
Be quiet; we will be fine.	Silencio, todo va a salir bien.
Fire drill	Adiestramiento para incendio.
Walk quietly out of the building.	Salgan del edificio sin hacer ruido.

Stop at the fence.	Párense/Deténganse en la reja.
The firemen are watching.	Los bomberos están mirando.
Be quiet.	En silencio.
Go quietly back to our classroom.	Regresen a la clase en silencio.
Code blue/red (intruder)	Código azul/rojo (intruso)
I have to lock the door to keep us safe.	Tengo que cerrar la puerta con llave para estar seguros.
I will close the blinds.	Cerraré las persianas.
I will turn off the lights.	Voy a apagar las luces.
We have to go over there and sit on the floor.	Tenemos que ir allí y sentarnos en el suelo.
When we hear the all clear, return to your seats.	Cuando escuchemos que ya todo pasó, pueden regresar a sus asientos.
This is practice.	Esta es una práctica.

Cognates

Nouns

code	código
cafeteria	cafetería
computer lab	centro de computadoras
gymnasium	gimnasio
intruder	intruso
laboratory	laboratorio
office	oficina
parking lot	parqueo
science	ciencias
silence	silencio

Verbs

count	contar
return	retornar

CHAPTER 5

GETTING ACADEMIC: READING, WRITING, MATH, SOCIAL STUDIES, AND SCIENCE

Reading

Okay, it's time for reading groups. What group am I in?	Bueno, es la hora de los grupos de lectura. ¿En qué grupo estoy?
Maria, you are in the group with Juan and Ana.	María, tú estás en el grupo de Juan y Ana.
Your group table is in the front of the room.	La mesa de tu grupo está al frente de la clase.

Math

Get out your math book and a piece of paper.	Saca tu libro de matemáticas y un papel.
What does my math book look like?	¿Cómo es mi libro de matemáticas?
Ask your buddy Sam. He will show you.	Pregúntale a tu compañero Sam. El te va a enseñar.
Remember that we added the milk cartons yesterday?	¿Recuerdas que sumamos los cartones de leche ayer?
How many did you have?	¿Cuántos tenías?
Your group had the most.	Tu grupo tenía más.
Your group had the least.	Tu grupo tenía menos.
Right! Now we are going to make a graph with that information.	¡Correcto! Ahora vamos a hacer un gráfico con esa información.

Science

Each group has a set of pictures of flowers.	Cada grupo tiene un juego de fotos de flores.
We are going to practice our observation steps and skills.	Vamos a seguir los pasos y a practicar nuestras destrezas.
Here are magnifying glasses for each of you.	Aquí están las lupas para cada uno de ustedes.
Okay, use the lenses to examine the flowers.	Muy bien, usen los lentes para examinar las flores.
What do you see?	¿Qué ven?
Write what you see in the place on the worksheet.	Escriban lo que ven en el lugar correcto en la hoja de ejercicios.

Writing

We had macaroni and cheese.	Comimos macarrones con queso.
That's great! But let's talk about words that can describe food.	¡Qué bien! Pero hablemos de las palabras que pueden describir la comida.
Words that describe something are called adjectives.	Las palabras que describen algo se llaman adjetivos.
Here are some good ones.	Aquí hay algunas buenas.
Delicious, crunchy, sweet, hot, spicy, cold, yummy, yucky.	Delicioso, crujiente, dulce, caliente, picante, frío, rico, feo.
I will write them on the overhead.	Los voy a escribir en el proyector.
Now as a class, let's write a sentence about dinner using one or two of those words.	Ahora entre todos, vamos a escribir una oración acerca de la comida usando una o dos de estas palabras.
Okay, now everyone write your own descriptive sentences.	Bueno, ahora cada uno escribe sus propias oraciones descriptivas.
Write four sentences using at least two adjectives in each sentence.	Escriban cuatro oraciones usando por lo menos dos adjetivos en cada oración.

Remember to use your best penmanship and punctuation.	Recuerden usar buena letra y la puntuación correcta.
We are going to write about what we had last night for dinner.	Vamos a escribir acerca de lo que comimos anoche.

Language Structure: Past Tense With Irregular Verbs

Saber (to know)	**Hacer** (to do)	**Dar** (to give)	**Poder** (to be able to)	**Poner** (to put)
supe	hice	di	pude	puse
supiste	hiciste	diste	pudiste	pusiste
supo	hizo	dio	pudo	puso
supimos	hicimos	dimos	pudimos	pusimos
supisteis	hicisteis	disteis	pudisteis	pusisteis
supieron	hicieron	dieron	pudieron	pusieron

Ir (to go)	**Ser** (to be)	**Estar** (to be)	**Tener** (to have)	**Conducir** (to drive)
fui	fui	estuve	tuve	conduje
fuiste	fuiste	estuviste	tuviste	condujiste
fue	fue	estuvo	tuvo	condujo
fuimos	fuimos	estuvimos	tuvimos	condujimos
fuisteis	fuisteis	estuvisteis	tuvisteis	condujisteis
fueron	fueron	estuvieron	tuvieron	condujeron

Venir (to come)	**Decir** (to say/tell)	**Traducir** (to translate)	**Traer** (to bring)
vine	dije	traduje	traje
viniste	dijiste	tradujiste	trajiste
vino	dijo	tradujo	trajo
vinimos	dijimos	tradujimos	trajimos
vinisteis	dijisteis	tradujisteis	trajisteis
vinieron	dijeron	tradujeron	trajeron

Querer (to love/want)
quise
quisiste
quiso
quisimos
quisisteis
quisieron

Schedule and Subjects

How to question and address more than one student:

It's time for____	Es la hora de____
math	matemáticas
reading/writing	lectura/escritura
science	ciencias
social studies	ciencias sociales
Get our your science book.	Saquen sus libros de ciencias.
What ways can you describe it?	¿Cómo lo pueden describir?
How can we add those up?	¿Cómo podemos sumar?
Let's count together.	Vamos a contar.
Let's count by 2's, 5's, 10's.	Contemos de dos en dos, de cinco en cinco, de dies en dies.

Content Area Vocabulary

Math   Reading to one student:

addition	suma	Follow along.	Sigue.
subtraction	resta	What is the sound?	¿Cuál es el sonido?
factors	factores	This word is____	Esta palabra es____
reduce	reducir	This letter is____	Esta letra es____
left over	residuo	Find the beginning.	Encuentra el comienzo.
multiply	multiplicar	Stretch the sounds.	Alarga los sonidos.
How many?	¿cuántos?		
percent	por ciento		
equal	igual		
pattern	patrón		

Language Arts

Who was the main character?	¿Quién era el personaje principal?
What was the setting?	¿Cuál fue el escenario?

How do you know?	¿Cómo lo sabes?
Think of words that are interesting.	Piensa en palabras interesantes.
Describe your ideas.	Describe tus ideas.
These are descriptive words.	Estas son palabras descriptivas.
Use your best penmanship.	Usa buena letra.
Remember punctuation.	Recuerda la puntuación.
Use the word wall.	Usa la lista de palabras.
Use correct spelling.	Usa ortografía correcta.

Science

Observe/Look at	Observa/Mira
What is the same?	¿Cuál es igual?
Find a pattern	Encuentra un patrón.
Weigh the____	Pesa el/la____
Add one drop.	Añade una gota.
Identify the material.	Identifica el material.
Use your senses.	Usa tus sentidos.
Record your data.	Anota los datos.
Share the materials.	Comparte los materiales.
Discuss the results.	Discute los resultados.
What is your hypothesis?	¿Cuál es tu hipótesis?
What is your conclusion?	¿Cuál es tu conclusión?

Cognates

Nouns		Verbs	
adjectives	adjetivos	add	añade
cartons	cartones	describe	describe
conclusion	conclusión	discuss	discute
figures	figuras	examine	examina
flowers	flores	count	cuenta
graph	gráfico	observe	observa
hypothesis	hipótesis	**Adjectives**	
ideas	ideas		
information	información	descriptive	descriptivo
letter	letra	crunchy	crujiente
materials	materiales	delicious	delicioso
mathematics	matemáticas	interesting	interesante
multiplication	multiplicación	magnificent	magnífico
percent	porciento	**Adverbs**	
projector	proyector		
punctuation	puntuación	at the front	al frente
sound	sonido		
subtraction	sustracción		

CHAPTER 6

HANDLING ILLNESSES AND FIRST AID

In the Nurse's Office
Student Has a Sore Tooth

What's wrong, sweetie?	¿Qué te pasa hijito/hijita?
This tooth hurts a lot.	Me duele esta muela mucho.
How much does it hurt? Does it hurt a lot or a little?	¿Cuánto te duele? ¿Te duele mucho o poco?
A lot/a little	Mucho/poco
We are going to call your parents.	Vamos a llamar a tus padres.
Are you going to call my mom or my dad's job?	¿Va a llamar al trabajo de mi mamá o al de mi papá?

Student Has a Stomachache

Do you want to go to the bathroom?	¿Quieres ir al baño?
No, thank you.	No, gracias.

Student Has an Unidentified Problem

What's wrong?	¿Qué te pasa?
It hurts here.	Me duele aquí.
Come, lie down on the bed.	Ven, acuéstate en la cama.

Student Fell On the Playground

Miss Atkins, Roberto fell and he is bleeding.	Señorita Atkins, Roberto se hacaídoy le está saliendo sangre.
Oh, no! Where is he?	¡Ay no! ¿Dónde está?
Outside on the playground	Afuera en el patio
Roberto, what happened to you?	Roberto, hijito, ¿qué te pasó?
I can't move my foot.	No puedo mover el pie.
Laura, run to the office and tell the principal to call an ambulance.	Laura, corre a la oficina y dile a la directora que llame una ambulancia.

Student Facing General Health and Safety Challenges

What's wrong?	¿Qué te pasa?
What happened to you?	¿Qué te pasó?
My child	Hijito/hijita
Do you want____?	¿Quieres____?
Go to the bathroom.	Ve al baño.
Go to the nurse's office.	Anda a la enfermería
We're going to call____	Vamos a llamar____
It hurts.	Me duele.
I am going to take you.	Te voy a llevar.
fell	Se cayó.
has fallen	Se ha caído.
lie down	Acuéstate.
is vomiting	Está vomitando.
is bleeding	Le está saliendo sangre.
You don't feel well?	¿No te sientes bien?
You can go.	Puedes ir.
You cannot go.	No puedes ir.
Are you dizzy?	¿Estás mareado/a?

Can you walk?	¿Puedes caminar?
Can you move your foot?	¿Puedes mover el pie?
Have some water.	Toma un poco de agua.

 ¡Ojo! Commands *ve* and *anda* are interchangeable. Both mean *"go"*.

Preadolescents and Other Health Issues

How to address one student:

Are you OK?	¿Estás bien?
You seem uncomfortable /ill.	Parece que estás incómoda/ incómodo/mal.
Do you have cramps?	¿Te duele el estómago?
Do you need to see the nurse?	¿Necesitas ver a la enfermera?
Do you need a sanitary napkin?	¿Necesitas una toalla higiénica?
Are you having your period?	¿Estás con la regla?

Health-Related Words Vocabulary

the tooth	la muela
the nurse's office	la enfermería
job	el trabajo
tummy	la barriga
doctor	el doctor
medical insurance	el seguro médico
the foot	el pie
bed	la cama
honey/endearment	mi amor
today	hoy
up	arriba
here	aquí
why?	¿por qué?

Courtesy Instructions

Let me feel your forehead.	Déjame tocarte la frente.
Remember to use a Kleenex to blow your nose	Acuérdate de usar un pañuelo de papel para limpiarte la nariz.
Wash your hands after you use the bathroom.	Lávate las manos después de usar el baño.
You can put your head down on the desk.	Puedes poner la cabeza en el escritorio.

Question Words

Where?	¿Dónde?
How much?	¿Cuánto?
What?	¿Qué?
Why?	¿Por qué?
Who?	¿Quién?
Which?	¿Cuál?

Cognates

Nouns

ambulance	ambulancia
director	director
doctor	doctor
exam	examen
infirmary	enfermería
mom	mamá
office	oficina
papa	papá
patio	patio
scale	escala
student	estudiante

Verbs

to move	mover
to preoccupied/ to worry	preocuparse
to serve	servir
to use	usar
to vomit	vomitar

Adjectives

much	mucho

Parent Calls From Home
Student Has an Upset Stomach

Parent: Hello, this is Juana Nuñez speaking, _____Nuñez's mother.	Buenos Días, le habla Juana Nuñez, la mamá de _____ Nuñez.
Teacher: Yes, how can I help you?	Sí, ¿en qué puedo servirle?
Parent: My son/daughter is vomiting and can't attend school today.	Mi hijo/hija está vomitando y no puede asistir a la escuela hoy.
Teacher: Oh, I am sorry. Are you taking him/her to the doctor?	¡Ay que pena! ¿Lo/la va a llevar al doctor?
Parent: No, because we don't have either money or medical insurance.	No, porque no tenemos ni dinero ni seguro médico.

Student Is Absent

Parent: May I speak to Mr. Martin, please?	¿Puedo hablar con el señor Martin, por favor?
Teacher: Speaking.	El habla.
Parent: Good morning, Mr. Martin. This is Jose Durango speaking.	Señor Martin, buenos días. Le habla José Durango.
Teacher: Good morning, Mr. Durango. How may help you?	Buenos días, Sr. Durango. ¿En qué le puedo servir?
Parent: My son/daughter can't make it to school today and he/she has a test today, right?	Mi hijo/hija no puede ir a la escuela y hoy tiene un examen, ¿no?
Teacher: Why can't he come?	¿Por qué no puede venir?
Parent: Because he/she fell yesterday and he/she can't walk.	Porque se cayó anoche y no puede caminar.
Teacher: Don't worry, I can give him/her the test when he/she comes back.	No se preocupe, le puedo tomar el examen cuando vuelva.
Parent: Thanks a lot, sir.	Muchísimas gracias, señor.

Language Structure: Imperfect Mood (Past)

In Spanish, there are two kinds of simple past tenses: preterite and imperfect. We introduced the preterite in the previous lesson. We will introduce the imperfect here. Endings for regular ar verbs are: *aba, abas, aba, ábamos, ábais, aban*. Endings for er and ir verbs are identical: *ía, ías, ía, íamos, ían*. The difference between the preterite and imperfect is that the preterite expresses a completed action, while the imperfect was an ongoing and habitual action in the past. The imperfect is equivalent to *I used to* in English, and it can also be equivalent to the past progressive *I was doing* my homework.

Frequent expressions with the imperfect mood:

todos los sábados *every Saturday*
con frecuencia *frequently*
habitualmente *habitually*
a veces *sometimes*

siempre *always*
a menudo *often*
generalmente *usually*
casi todos los domingos *almost every Sunday*

Preterite Imperfect

I **played** volleyball yesterday.
Jugué vóleibol ayer.

I **used to play** volleyball when I lived there.
Jugaba vóleibol cuando vivía allí.

They **ate** chicken yesterday.
Comieron pollo ayer.

They **were eating** chicken when I arrived.
Comían pollo cuando llegué.

Regular verbs

"Ar" endings:		"Er" endings:		"Ir" endings:	
Cantar *(to sing)*		**Aprender** *(to learn)*		**Permitir** *(to allow)*	
cant**aba**	cant**ábamos**	aprend**ía**	aprend**íamos**	permit**ía**	permit**íamos**
cant**abas**	cant**ábais**	aprend**ías**	aprend**íais**	permit**ías**	permit**íais**
cant**aba**	cant**aban**	aprend**ía**	aprend**ían**	permit**ía**	permit**ían**

 ¡Ojo! Almost all verbs are regular in the imperfect. There are only three irregular verbs:

Ir *(to go)*		Ver *(to see)*		Ser *(to be)*	
Iba	íbamos	veía	veíamos	era	éramos
Ibas	ibais	veías	veíais	eras	érais
Iba	iban	veía	veían	era	eran

Examples:

Mis padres **iban** a la iglesia todos los domingos cuando yo era niña.
My parents went to church every Sunday when I was a girl.

CHAPTER 7

TALKING
WITH
FAMILIES

In the Spanish-speaking world, people always address adults with a title, such as Señor, Señorita, or Señora, rather than using a first name, while American people simply use the first name in most situations. Therefore, it is very unusual for Spanish speakers to hear themselves addressed by their first name in place of a title. Accordingly, instead of addressing a parent by his/her name, he/she should be addressed as Señor/Señora. A single woman is addressed as Señorita.

Additionally, in the Spanish-speaking world people say "hello" and "good-bye" with one or two kisses—with one kiss in most Latin American countries and with two kisses in Spain and Paraguay. Girls kiss other girls or boys as a friendship sign rather than a romantic relationship. Americans tend to keep more distance than Hispanics.

Parents Call In About Their Student
Student Was Unable to Complete Homework

Mom: Good morning, Miss. My son/daughter couldn't do homework last night because he/she had an upset stomach.	Mamá: Buenos Días, Señorita. Mi hijo/hija no pudo hacer la tarea anoche porque estuvo con dolor de estómago.
Teacher: It's all right, Madame. Don't worry. I hope your son/daughter gets better soon so that he/she can come back to school.	Está bien, señora, no se preocupe. Espero que su hijo/hija se mejore pronto para que vuelva a la escuela.

A Student Feels Ill and Needs to Go Home

Teacher: May I speak with Mrs. Meléndez, please?	¿Puedo hablar con la señora Meléndez?
Parent: Yes, Mrs. Parker, this is she speaking.	Si, señora Parker, con ella habla.
Teacher: I'm calling from Perkins School. Your son doesn't feel well. His ear hurts. And he is crying Can you come and pick him up?	Le hablo de la escuela Perkins. Su hijo Carlos no se siente bien. Le duele mucho el oído y está llorando. ¿Puede venir a recogerlo?
Parent: Yes, I'll be there in 30 minutes.	Sí, señorita. Estaré allí en treinta minutos.

Student Misbehaved

Teacher: Ms. Sánchez, this is Ms Coates speaking. Miguel misbehaved today. He has been sent to the principal's office Can you meet with me to talk about it?	Señora Sánchez, habla la señora Coates. Miguel no se portó bien hoy. Está castigado en la dirección. ¿Puede venir para hablar conmigo?
Parent: Oh, Ms. Coates, I am sorry. I am working and I can't leave until 3 in the afternoon.	¡Ay señorita Coates, que pena¡ Estoy trabajando y no puedo salir hasta las tres de la tarde.
Teacher: That is okay. When can you be here?	Está bien, señora. ¿A qué hora puede venir?

Student Left Jacket at School

Parent: Miss, my son left his jacket here yesterday. He says he left it in the classroom.	Señorita, mi hijo dejó su chaqueta aquí ayer. Dice que la dejó en su clase.
Teacher: Let me ask the janitors. Hold on, please.	Voy a preguntarle al personal de limpieza. Un momento, por favor.
Parent: Thank you very much, Miss.	Muchas gracias, señorita.

Student Did Not Return Report Card to School

Teacher: Hello, Mrs. Martinez, please.	Aló/Bueno, ¿Con la señor Martinez, por favor?
Parent: Speaking.	Ella habla.
Teacher: Madame, this is Nancy's teacher speaking.	Señora, le habla la maestra de Nancy.
Parent: Good morning, Ms. Johnson.	Buenos días, señorita Johnson.
Teacher: How are you? I am calling because Nancy didn't bring back her report card signed.	Cómo está usted? La llamo porque Nancy no ha traído su libreta de notas firmada.

Language Structure: Present Perfect Tense

In English, the present perfect tense is used to express an indefinite past action or an action that started in the past and it is still relevant in the present.

For example:

I have studied Spanish for two years

He estudiado español por dos años

Have you had breakfast yet?

¿Has desayunado ya?

Charlar *(to chat)*	**Comprender** *(to learn)*	**Vivir** *(to live)*
he charl**ado**	**he** comprend**ido**	**he** viv**ido**
has charl**ado**	**has** comprend**ido**	**has** viv**ido**
ha charl**ado**	**ha** comprend**ido**	**ha** viv**ido**
hemos charl**ado**	**hemos** comprend**ido**	**hemos** viv**ido**
habéis charl**ado**	**habéis** comprend**ido**	**habéis** viv**ido**
han charl**ado**	**han** comprend**ido**	**han** viv**ido**

How to form the present perfect tense

The verb *haber* works as an auxiliary verb and needs to be conjugated: *he, has, ha, hemos, habéis, han*. It works with the past participle form of the main verb. The verb *haber* is used in place of "have" in English.

With regular verbs ending in **ar**:

conversar convers + **ado**

Verbs ending in **er** or **ir**:

perder perd + **ido**

compartir compart + **ido**

There are some irregular past participles:

abrir Abierto (opened)
cubrir cubierto (covered)
decir dicho (said)
escribir escrito (written)

hacer hecho (done)
morir muerto (died)
poner puesto (put)
resolver resuelto (resolved)

romper roto (broken)
ver visto (seen)
volver vuelto (come back)

¡Ojo! Past participles can work as adjectives in the sentence when used with the verb *estar*. In this case the subject agrees in gender and number with the past participle or adjective.

For example:

La puer**ta** está abier**ta.**
La ventan**a** está rota.

The door is open.
The window is broken.

Politeness

There are three ways to say "I am sorry." *Disculpa* means: "It is my fault/pardon."
¡Qué pena! can also be used to apologize. *Lo siento* and *¡que pena!* convey sympathy or empathy about what has happened or what was said.

Please	Por favor
Thank you very much	Muchas gracias
I am sorry.	Disculpa
Could you?	¿Podrías?
I am sorry.	¡Qué pena¡/Lo siento.

When a Student is in Trouble

to behave/ misbehave	portarse bien/mal	Your child is in trouble.	Su hijo/hija se portó mal.
punished	castigado	_____is punished	_____está castigado/castigada.
leave	dejar	Leave your jacket.	Deja tu chaqueta.
speak	hablar	Speak slowly.	Habla despacio.
wait	esperar	Wait for me.	Espérame.
call	llamar	Call your mom.	Llama a tu mamá.
work	trabajar	Where does he work?	¿Dónde trabaja?
ask	preguntar	Ask your parents.	Pregúntales a tus padres.
to be	estar	Where's your dad?	¿Dónde está tu papá?

The Essential Spanish Phrase Book for Teachers

be able to	poder	Were you able to understand?	¿Pudiste comprender?
pick up	recoger	Pick up the candy wrapping.	Recoge la envoltura del dulce.
come	venir	Is your mom coming?	¿Viene tu mamá?
to feel good/bad	sentirse bien/mal	Do you feel bad?	¿Te sientes mal?
today	hoy	Did you do your homework today?	¿Hiciste tu tarea hoy?
yesterday	ayer	Were you absent yesterday?	¿Faltaste ayer?

Cognates

Nouns

class	la clase
hello	hola
hello (on the phone)	aló/bueno
hour	hora
immediate	inmediato
minute	minuto
personnel	personal
recess	recreo
stomach	estómago
school	escuela

Content words

mom/mother	mamá/madre
dad/father	papá/padre
teacher	maestro/a
the homework	la tarea
the report card	la libreta de notas
cleaning staff	personal de limpieza
someone's address	la dirección de alguien

CHAPTER 8

SUPPORTING FAMILY CONFERENCES

Hispanic families value education for their children but see it as the job of the teachers, who are trained and educated. Accordingly, it is important to help them understand that in the United States both parents and teachers work together on their students' education.

All families may need reminders of the time for their conference. Below is a form in English and repeated in Spanish that could be used to communicate with the families so that attendance is encouraged.

Student's Name_____

The date and time of your conference at school is _____

Parent, teacher conferences are very important for your child's success in school.

Please arrive at least 10 minutes early so that we can stay on schedule. Come to the classroom and wait in the hall.

If you need an interpreter, please call the school 2 days before the conference. The telephone number is _____. I am looking forward to seeing you and discussing your child's interests and progress.

Here is the same form in Spanish.

Nombre del niño o niña _____

La fecha y hora de la reunión en la escuela es _____

Las reuniones de maestros con los padres de familia son muy importantes para el éxito de su niño/niña en la escuela.

Favor de llegar por lo menos 10 minutos antes para poder mantener nuestro horario. Venga a la clase y espere en el pasillo.

Si necesita un intérprete, por favor llame a la escuela dos días antes de la reunión. El número de teléfono es _____. Espero verlos para poder hablar sobre los intereses y el progreso de su niño/niña.

The Essential Spanish Phrase Book for Teachers

Some schools send report cards home with the students or mail them before the conference. Others hand them out during the conference. Whatever the practice, it is important to let the parents know what the reports mean. Or ask them to bring the report to the conference so they can ask questions about it. Some districts are now focusing on building relationships with families at the conference rather than focusing on grades. In that case, some of the phrases in the first chapters of this book can be used to get to know one another.

Phrases to Use During the Conference

Hello Mr. and Mrs. _____·You are _____ parents?	Hola señor y señora _____· ¿Ustedes son los padres de_____?
Please sit down here.	Por favor siéntense aquí.
How are both of you? Okay?	¿Cómo están ustedes? ¿Bien?
I am so glad that you could come for the conference. It is very important for your child's progress.	Estoy muy contento/a de que pudieron venir. Es muy importante para el progreso de su niño/niña.
I enjoy having _____ in class.	Disfruto de tener a _____ en la clase.
What does he/she say about school?	¿Qué dice él/ella de la escuela?
Positive Remarks	**Notas Positivas**
He/She is eager to learn.	El/Ella tiene ansias de aprender.
He/She has tried very hard to learn.	El/Ella ha hecho un gran esfuerzo por aprender.
This is the progress report for ___	Estas son las notas de ___
This is a portfolio of his/her papers.	Este es el portafolio de sus trabajos.
His/Her best subject is math, writing, reading, English.	Su mejor asignatura es matemáticas, escritura, lectura, inglés.
What does he/she like the best?	¿Qué le gusta más a él/ella?
He/She always pays attention.	El/Ella siempre presta atención.

He/She is always polite and helpful.	El/Ella siempre es muy cortés y le gusta ayudar.
He/She has done well up to now in math, but I think the next unit might be a challenge.	El/Ella está bien en matemáticas hasta ahora, pero pienso que la próxima unidad podría ser un desafío.
At the beginning of the year, his/her writing was like this….Now we see many improvements.	Al comienzo del año, su escritura era así. Ahora vemos que es mucho mejor.
He/She is now able to answer my questions in English.	El/Ella puede responder a mis preguntas en inglés ahora.
He/She will be able to speak English fluently very soon.	El/Ella podrá hablar inglés con fluidez muy pronto.
Do all of you speak some English at home?	¿Ustedes hablan un poco de inglés en casa?
Not So Positive Remarks	**Notas No Tan Positivas**
He/She struggles with math, reading, spelling.	Él/Ella lucha con las matemáticas, lectura y ortografía.
He/She does not speak loudly enough in class, so it is difficult for me to know if he/she is correct.	El/Ella no habla lo suficientemente recio/fuerte en clase, entonces es difícil saber si ha contestado bien.
He/She does not ask questions always, so I don't know what he/she doesn't understand.	El/Ella no hace preguntas, así que no siempre sé lo que no comprende.
If I ask him to repeat something, he/she thinks he is wrong and won't try again.	Si le hago repetir algo, piensa que está equivocado/equivocada, y no repite de nuevo.
Please tell him/her that it is important to speak more loudly in school so that he/she can be heard by the teacher.	Por favor, dígale que es importante hablar más alto en la escuela para poder ser escuchado/escuchada por el maestro/la maestra.
His/her spelling grade is low. Does he/she study at home?	Su nota de ortografía es baja. ¿Estudia en la casa?

Study Habits at Home	Hábitos de Estudio en Casa
Does he/she have a place to do homework?	¿Tiene un lugar donde hacer su tarea?
Does he/she have older siblings who can help with homework?	¿Tiene hermanos mayores que pueden ayudar con la tarea?
Is there a set time each day to do homework?	¿Hay una hora fija cada día para hacer la tarea?
What time does he/she go to bed?	¿A qué hora se acuesta?
Is there enough time to do the work at home?	¿Hay suficiente tiempo para hacer el trabajo en casa?

A Note About Language and Culture:
Using an Interpreter

This can take many forms in a school setting. Sometimes, a family will bring a friend or older sibling to interpret for them. Sometimes schools are able to provide interpreters. If so, it is important to think about how to change your communication style and pace in order for everyone to understand what is being said. There are several sites on the Internet that provide hints about using interpreters, but some basics are below.

One useful site is from the University of South Carolina Center for Child and Family Services; the address is: www.sc.edu/ccfs/education/NewHABLA/InterpreterTips.htm.

Just because someone can speak two languages does not mean that he or she is capable of interpreting. This is especially true of those brought in by the family. Interpreting requires the ability to listen carefully to two people, as well as proficiency in two languages. Before you start, introduce everyone to each other. If the interpreter is provided by the district, he or she may be familiar with the typical topics covered in a conference. However, if you can provide in advance a list of topics, or jargon that you will be using, it will help the interpreter prepare.

If it is possible, position the interpreter beside the parents. If you are using an interpreter from the district, it is important to say that all the information will be kept confidential.
Look at the parents when you speak, not the interpreter. Ask the interpreter to use first person for translation so that it will be a more direct communication. For example, instead of saying, "Tell her that I enjoy having Alicia in class," say, "I enjoy having Alicia in class," as you are looking at the parents. That way, the interpreter can fade into the background and serve as a conduit for information. This might change if the interpreter is a family member.

Before you begin, discuss with the interpreter whether the interpretation will be consecutive or simultaneous. Regardless, be sure to speak slowly and distinctly. If the translation is consecutive, you should pause after every sentence or complete thought so that the interpreter can proceed. Remember that the translation of what you said may take longer in Spanish. Likewise, any questions the parents have might sound longer than what the interpreter says to you. English is a somewhat direct language and sometimes it takes fewer words to get the point across.

Try to avoid using highly technical language or educational jargon. It may not translate correctly or the interpreter may not know the terms. Avoid puns and jokes for the same reason. It is polite to pause frequently to ask the parents if they have any questions. However, some families feel that out of respect, they should not question the teacher. Try to impress on them that you welcome questions and want to meet the needs of their child. It is also polite to ask the interpreter if he or she needs a break or to let you know if you should slow down or speed up.

If appropriate, make use of diagrams or lists. If you have given the parents some suggestions for improving homework or other written or verbal information, ask them to repeat the instructions back to you so that you can clear up any misunderstanding immediately.

It is important to make adjustments in your schedule to accommodate the longer time required for a bilingual conference. Remember that few other cultures focus on being "on time" the way mainstream USA does. If you do run out of time, apologize and reschedule for another time to continue your discussion.

Cognates

Nouns		Adjectives	
habits	hábitos	difficult	difícil
interests	intereses	fixed	fijo
interpreter	intérprete		
portfolio	portafolio		
positive	positivo		
progress	progreso		
report	reporte		
reunion/ meeting	reunión		
study	estudio		

Appendix

The phrases used in this book are not in any particular tense or order, but they are arranged by topics, and reflect typical speech patterns of most teachers in the United States. We recommend formal study of Spanish so that you may gain full understanding of the language and its cultural aspects.

Recommendations: How to Learn Spanish

Spanish textbooks
Tapes/CDs
Music
DVD movies
Spanish Internet pages
Spanish radio stations
Spanish channels: Univision, Telemundo, Telesur, etc.
Visits with native Spanish speakers
Prolonged visits to Spanish-speaking countries and participation in Spanish language institutes

Cognates List

Nouns

accident	accidente	colors	colores
activity	actividad	computer lab	centro de cómputo
adjectives	adjetivos	computers	computadoras
ambulance	ambulancia	conclusion	conclusion
babies	bebés	counselor	consejero
blouse	blusa	day	día
bus	autobus	diary	diario
cafeteria	cafeteria	director	director
carton	carton	doctor	doctor
chocolate	chocolate	exam	examen
circle	círculo	fault	falta
class	clase	figures	figures
code	código	flowers	flores

graph	gráfico	parents	padres
gymnasium	gimnasio	parking lot	parqueo
hello	hola/aló	percent	porciento
home	hogar	permission	permiso
hypothesis	hipótesis	personnel	personal
ideas	ideas	photo	foto
infirmary	enfermería	plate	plato
information	información	poem	poema
immediate	inmediato	possible	posible
instructions	instrucciones	practice	práctica
intruder	intruso	projector	proyector
is	es	punctuation	puntuación
laboratory	laboratorio	recess	recreo
language	lenguaje	rules	reglas
leader	líder	scale	escala
letter/alphabet	letra	school	escuela
line	línea	science	ciencias
list	lista	silence	silencio
materials	materiales	sir	señor
mathematics	matemáticas	sound	sonido
minute	minuto	stomach	estómago
mom	mamá	story	historia
multiplication	multiplicación	student	estudiante
music	música	subtraction	sustracción
note	nota	sweater	suéter
office	oficina	time	tiempo
order	orden	turn	turno
others	otros	voice	voz
pants	pantalones		
papa	papá		

Verbs

calm down	cálmate			
cooperate	coopera			
count	cuenta			
describe	describe			
examine	examina			
let's count	contemos			
move	mueve			
observe	observa			
needs	necesita			
pass out	pasen			
[pay] attention	[presta] atención			
preoccupy	preocupa			
respond	responde			
return	retorna			
serve	sirve			
touch	toca			
use	usa			
vomit	vomita			

Adjective

much	mucho

Adverbs

no	no
Oh no!	¡Ay no!

Pronouns

me	mí

References

Dalbor, J. B. (1997). *Spanish pronunciation.* Fort Worth: Holt, Rinehart and Winston.

Lee, J. F. & Van Patten, B. (2003). *Making communicative language teaching happen.* Boston: McGraw-Hill.

Mohr, K. A. J. & Mohr, E. S. (2007). Extending english-language learners' classroom interactions using the Response Protocol. *The Reading Teacher, 60*(5), 440–450.

Internet Resources

www.colorincolorado.org/educators/background/cognates

www.colorincolorado.org/pdfs/articles/cognates.pdf

www.sc.edu/ccfs/education/NewHABLA/InterpreterTips.htm